Little Prayers For Little Hearts

By Gayatri Shinde

"Little Prayers for Little Hearts"

INTRODUCTION

Welcome to "Little Prayers for Little Hearts"!

Dear Parents and Caregivers,
Thank you for choosing "Little Prayers for Little Hearts" to share with your child. This book is a special collection of simple, heartfelt prayers designed to introduce young children to the beauty, comfort, and power of prayer. Each prayer is accompanied by vibrant and engaging illustrations, making it easier for your child to connect with the messages and find joy in their daily prayers.

MORNING GLORY

Good morning, Lord,
it's time to rise,
The sun is shining in
the skies.
Thank you for this
brand-new day,
Guide my steps and
lead my way.

A GRATEFUL HEART

Thank you, God,
for this new dawn,
For birds that sing
and the fresh, green lawn.
Help me be grateful,
kind, and true,
In everything
I say and do

A JOYFUL DAY

Good morning, God, I'm wide awake,
Thank you for this day you make.
Help me laugh and help me play,
And spread your joy in every way.

A DAY OF GIVING

Good morning, Lord, help me today,
To give in every little way.
With acts of kindness, big and small,
Let me spread your love to all.

A DAY OF LOVE

Dear God above, please hear my prayer,
Guide me with your loving care.
Help me be kind, and help me be strong,
To do what's right, not what's wrong.

A PRAYER FOR REPENTANCE

Dear God, I'm sorry for my wrong,
Help me be honest, brave, and strong.
Forgive my sins and guide my way,
In your love, I'll always stay.

A Happy Heart

Morning light, morning cheer,
Thank you, God, for being near.
Help me smile, help me sing,
Guide me through this day, dear King.

A LEARNING PRAYER

Thank you, Lord, for this new day,
For time to learn and time to play.
Help me listen, help me grow,
Teach me things I need to know.

A PRAYER
FOR STRENGTH

Lord, I rise to greet the day,
Guide me in your perfect way.
Give me strength and give me cheer,
To face this day without a fear.

LOVE AND CARE

Love and care are always near,
In every hug, in every cheer.
They make the world a nicer place,
With every smile, in every face.

LOVE FOR ALL

Thank you, God, for love so true,
Help me share it in all I do.
With family, friends, and those I see,
Let your love flow through me.

LOVING ACTIONS

Dear God, help my actions show,
The love you give and let it grow.
With every smile and every deed,
Help me be kind in word and seed.

A NEW BEGINNING

Good morning, God, I start anew,
With a heart that's clean and true.
Forgive my past, help me grow,
In your love, let kindness show.

SHARING LOVE

Thank you, God, for love so dear,
Help me share it, far and near.
With every smile and hug I give,
Show your love in how I live.

A PRAYER FOR KIND HEARTS

Dear Lord, help my heart today,
To be kind in every way.
With every smile and every deed,
Let your love be all I need.

LOVE AND LIGHT

Dear God, your love is shining bright,
Help me share it with all my might.
With kindness, love, and gentle care,
Help me show your light everywhere.

SPREADING LOVE

Good morning, Lord, I thank you so,
For the love that helps me grow.
Guide my heart and guide my hands,
To spread your love across the lands.

A Prayer for Kind Words

Dear Lord, help my words today,
Be kind and gentle in every way.
Let them bring comfort,
Let them bring cheer,
To everyone, both far and near.

GRATEFUL JOURNEYS

Dear God, thank you for the fun,
For adventures beneath the sun.
For hikes and swims and games to play,
For every bright and happy day.

A Caring Heart

Thank you, God, for loving me,
Help my heart be kind and free.
To care for others, big and small,
And show your love to one and all.

A LOVING HEART

A loving heart will share a smile,
And sit with you to chat a while.
It comforts you when you feel blue,
And shows you love in all it does and do.

BIRTHDAY PRAYER

Dear God, today's a special day,
Thank you for my life, I pray.
Bless my year with love and cheer,
Guide me through another year.

CHRISTMAS PRAYER

Good morning, Lord,
It's Christmas Day,
Thank you for
Your love always.
Bless our home
With joy and peace,
Let your love in us increase.

THANK YOU FOR LOVE

Dear God, for love, I thank you so,
For the love that helps me grow.
For family, friends, and all I meet,
Thank you for this life so sweet.

A Prayer for Guidance

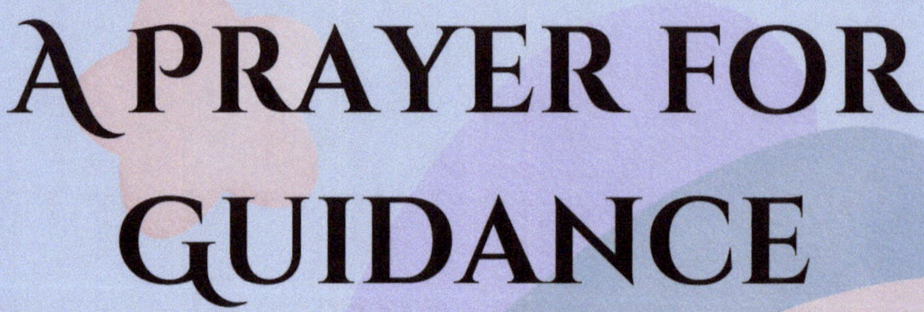

Good morning, God, I pray to you,
Guide me in all I say and do.
Protect me from the wrong I find,
With your love, keep me kind.

A Gentle Heart

A gentle heart is soft and bright,
It fills the world with pure delight.
With every hug and every cheer,
A gentle heart is always near.

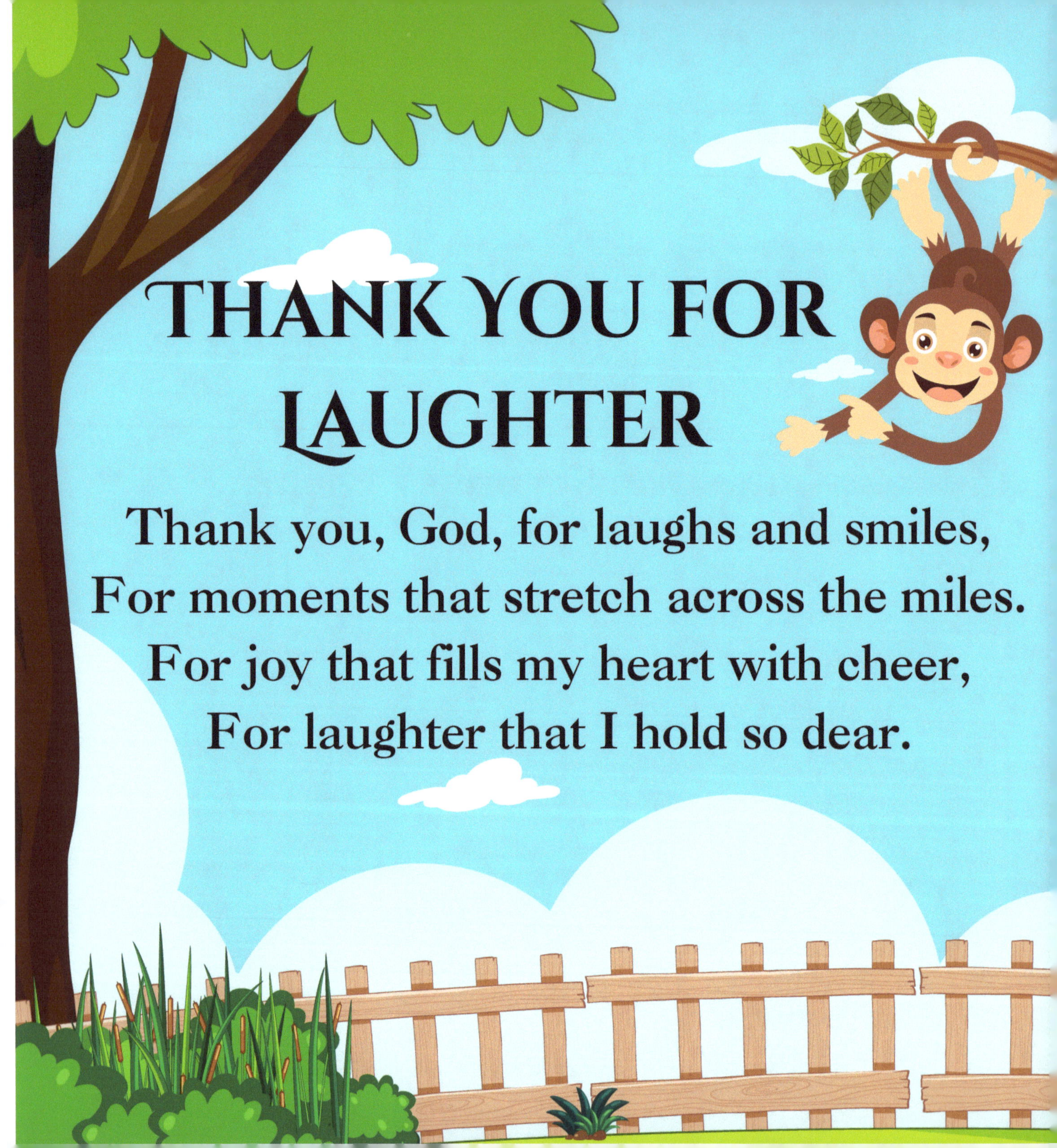

THANK YOU FOR LAUGHTER

Thank you, God, for laughs and smiles,
For moments that stretch across the miles.
For joy that fills my heart with cheer,
For laughter that I hold so dear.

GRATEFUL FOR FRIENDS

Thank you, God, for friends so true,
For fun and laughter, old and new.
For games we play and times we share,
Thank you, God, for being there.

A Heart Restored

Good morning, Lord, I come to you,
Asking for forgiveness true.
Restore my heart, make it new,
Help me live my life for you.

A KIND SOUL

A kind soul is a treasure, rare and true,
With every smile, it brightens the view.
It shares its warmth and spreads delight,
Turning dark days into light.

THANK YOU FOR MY HOME

Good morning, Lord, I'm thankful today,
For my home where I laugh and play.
For my bed where I sleep tight,
For my home, both day and night.

A HEART FULL OF LOVE

Dear Lord, fill my heart today,
With love that shines in every way.
Help me be kind, help me be true,
In all the things I say and do.

A KIND DAY

Thank you, God, for this new day,
Help me be kind in all I say.
With every person that I meet,
Let love and kindness guide my feet.

GRATEFUL FOR TODAY

Thank you, God, for this new day,
For your love in every way.
Guide me, help me, make me strong,
In your love, where I belong.

A LOVING DEED

Good morning, God, I start anew,
Help me show your love in all I do.
With helping hands and a caring heart,
Let your kindness be my part.

A Heart of Gold

A heart of gold will always share,
With gentle words and tender care.
It lifts you up when times are tough,
And gives you strength,
When things are rough.

THANK YOU FOR MY FAMILY

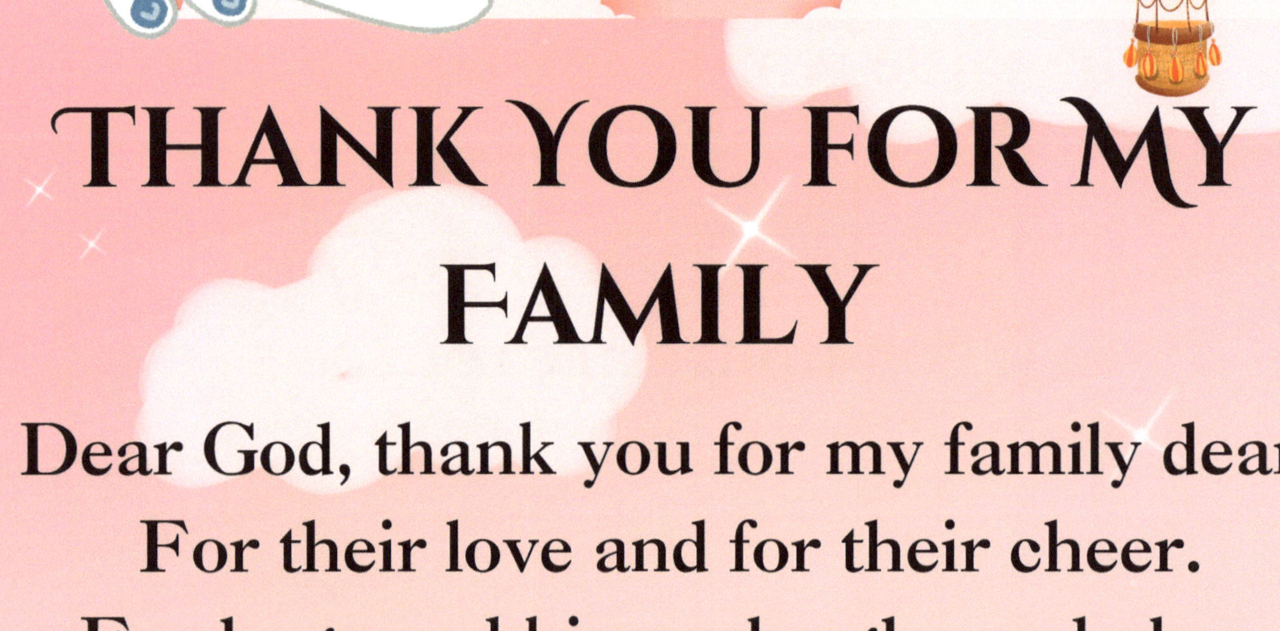

Dear God, thank you for my family dear,
For their love and for their cheer.
For hugs and kisses, laughs and play,
I'm grateful for them every day.

THANK YOU FOR NATURE

Dear Lord, I thank you for the trees,
For the buzzing bumblebees.
For mountains tall and oceans wide,
For every place where creatures hide.

A PRAYER FOR PEACE

Dear Lord, help me spread your peace,
In every way and every piece.
With loving thoughts and kind words too,
Help me always follow you.